LIVE EELS AND GRAND PIANOS

By Andrew Bradford

Published in 2011
by Callio Press, ISBN 978-0-85778-094-2
This paperback edition published by CallioViva
an imprint of CallioPress

37 Great Russell Street, London WC1B 3PP, United Kingdom
555 Fifth Avenue N.E. Suite 343, Saint Petersburg, Florida 33701,
USA
www.calliopress.com

ISBN 978-0-85778-094-2

Cover Design by Jag Lall

A CIP catalogue record for this book is available from
the British Library.
Available from CallioPress Online, all major online retailers
and available to order through your local bookshop.
Visit www.calliopress.com to buy our books
or email sales@calliopress.com

Printed and bound in the UK by The Callio Press Limited
Printed and bound in the USA by Entelyx International Inc.

This book is dedicated to all the survivors of Polio and their children

ANDREW BRADFORD

CONTENTS

ANDREW BRADFORD

CHAPTER 1

In the Playground

I was ten. I was in the playground of Fleecefield Primary School in Edmonton, North London. It was springtime in 1959. The small boy was in the year below me. I hardly knew him. I can't remember his name or what he looked like. But I will never forget the conversation.

'Your parents are cripple dicks, aren't they?' he said.

'They're not cripple dicks, they're disabled.' I replied.

'And when you grow up you'll be crippled too.'

'No I won't! My mum and dad have Polio – you catch that like a cold, you don't pass it on to your children!'

'Yes you do – my mum told me.'

I couldn't think of anything else to say. I hated his mother for her ignorance and prejudice. More than forty years later I stopped hating her and decided to write the story of my mum and dad, Charlie and Kathy Bradford. It's the story of their struggle to do the normal things that working class families did in the 1950s and 1960s. Things like earning a living, doing the housework, and all the humdrum things of family life that are usually taken for granted, such as the shopping, the gardening, going on holiday and going to see their son in the school play.

Charlie and Kathy couldn't take these things for granted, because since their early childhood they had both been severely disabled by Polio. For them, every one of these activities was a struggle. All they ever wanted was an ordinary family life, but for them to become ordinary they first had to become extraordinary. Not only did they have to overcome the physical obstacles, but they also had to overcome ignorance and prejudice.

But this is also the story of my childhood, and how my parents' disability affected me. Did I really reply to this small boy that my parents weren't cripple dicks, they were disabled? Had my parents, by the time I was nine, already found it necessary to explain the nature of the Polio virus, and re-assure me that I wouldn't be affected by it? I can't remember any such conversation with them; I just seemed to know these facts in the same way that I knew the way to school. Somehow I did know that this boy's mum was filling his head with nonsense. Poisonous, malicious, nonsense.

Before I introduce you to Charlie and Kathy, here is a very short history of the disease that caused their disabilities. Poliomyelitis, or Polio, is a viral infection spread by contaminated water or food. The only symptoms are headache, a sore throat and a high temperature, similar to flu. When it strikes adults or older children, most of them only suffer these mild flu-like symptoms, but in a minority of cases the virus escapes into the central nervous system and destroys myelin – the 'grey matter' that lines the spinal cord. As a result the motor neurones cease to send messages to the muscles in the lower body - usually just the limbs, but sometimes arms or the lungs - which then atrophy due to lack of stimulus.

Polio (which was known as Infantile Paralysis until the 1950s) first became a notifiable disease in England and Wales in 1912 - one year before Kathy caught the disease at the age of ten months, and three years after Charlie was attacked by the virus when he was three.

There were several epidemics in the United Kingdom between the turn of the century and the end of the Second World War, but in 1947 an unprecedented seven thousand cases were reported. Between 1947 and 1958 there were fifty-eight thousand cases, which left thirty-five thousand people disabled, and nearly four thousand dead. The disease was virtually eliminated in the developed world by the invention of a vaccine, followed by mass immunisation programmes in the late 1950s, but it still affects many people in Africa and the Indian sub-continent.

CHAPTER 2

Charlie

Edmonton is a north London suburb, although not a green middle-class commuter suburb. In the twentieth century it was a place where things such as food, furniture, electrical components and beer were made in large factories. These factories employed thousands of local people who lived in small Victorian terraces or council estates in the town. Charlie Bradford was born in Church Street, Edmonton in 1906. His dad, William, ran a fleet of horse drawn cabs from the family home next door to Lower Edmonton Station. When he was still in his teens William had walked to London from Brent Pelham, a tiny Hertfordshire village not far from Bishops Stortford. Edmonton was the first place in London he came to, and that's where he stayed for the rest of his life. Charlie's mother, Letitia Ford, was born in

Hatfield, Hertfordshire. Her parents had emigrated from Cork to escape the famine.

Charlie was the second youngest of six children, and contracted Polio when he was three. The disease had paralysed both legs; his left arm and he had a severe curvature of the spine. He was less than five feet tall. Until he was about fifty (when he started to use a wheelchair all the time) he walked with crutches and leg irons, and had to wear a leather and steel spinal corset that weighed nearly twenty pounds.

He was in and out of hospital, often for several months at a time, until he was twelve, so he had only two years of full-time education. When he wasn't in hospital, he was sometimes at home, and at other times he spent long periods being cared for by his paternal grandmother, Susan Bradford, at her cottage in Brent Pelham. He was a member of the Brent Pelham Scout Troop, and this is the earliest picture I have of him:

When Charlie left school at fourteen he was of course unemployable, so at various times in the 1920s and 1930s he peddled sweets from a hand-propelled wheelchair outside the local grammar school. He also made sandwiches that he sold to the men building the new A10 road, and bought second hand wheelchairs, which he reconditioned, and sold on to others.

After his mother died in 1926 his father remarried, and Charlie went to live with his brother Jack and Jack's wife Edith. Jack's main job was as a baker's roundsman, but at some time in the 1930s the two brothers went into business together, buying a corner shop on Hendon Road, Edmonton. Jack's daughter Kath (born in 1930) recalls:

'They both used to serve in the shop. They used to sell the Fantas drinks that were served from a big glass container with a tap on it. Jack used to bottle it up and sell it for a ha'penny a bottle. They also used to make their own ice cream. There used to be big blocks of ice delivered on a lorry and they crushed them up and mixed them with milk and custard powder.'

However, the shop was not a success, and after a few years they closed it. Jack's children recall that after it was closed Jack and Charlie bred wire–haired terriers to sell, and Charlie made jigsaw puzzles to sell in the market, before he returned to his pitch selling sweets outside the school.

Charlie was an activist for the rights of the disabled as early as the 1930s. He was asked by the Shaftesbury Society (a Christian charity) to help set up a 'cripple parlour' - a kind of self help group – in Edmonton. The group wrote letters to MPs about the financial consequences of disability. He (and countless others like him) couldn't afford to buy their crutches, leg irons and wheelchairs, so the society gave them lists of wealthy individuals they could write to, to ask them for financial support. In other words he had to write begging letters.

One of his benefactors was Mr. Street, a barrister from Surrey. Mr. Street was much older than Dad and they kept up a correspondence for forty years. They were still writing to each other when I was a teenager and Mr. Street was in his nineties. We didn't need his financial support by then, but these two men from such different backgrounds - Mr. Street still employed servants in the 1960s - had become friends. Every year when I was a boy he gave me a book for Christmas. The book arrived a few days before Christmas, together with a bottle of whisky for Charlie and a Christmas cake for Kathy from Harrods. Not many other houses on the council estate where we lived got a visit from the Harrods van. I still have the tattered and much read copy of 'Treasure Island' that he bought for me when I was seven, as well as several volumes by Dickens. I can't bring myself to throw them away.

At the start of World War II Charlie was living with his brother Jack and his family on Chiswick Road, Edmonton. My cousin Kath recalls:

'We had an outside Anderson shelter at the bottom of the garden. When there was an air-raid, no matter what time of day or night, Jack used to put Charlie on his back and take him to the shelter.'

After a few months of war, adults with disabilities were

evacuated from London. Charlie was sent to a 'cripple camp' at Dovercourt, Essex. That's where he met Kathleen Lines, a fellow evacuee.

CHAPTER 3

Kathy

Kathleen was born in Wandsworth, London in 1912. She was the eldest of six children; her youngest brother was only eight years younger than her. Her father, Henry Lines, was a French polisher who had married Beatrice Bridgeman the previous year. Both the Lines and Bridgeman families were military families, and both Henry and Beatrice had spent some of their youth in India.

Kathy caught the Polio virus when she was ten months old, and it left her disabled in both legs. When her mother was pregnant with her youngest son, her husband walked out of the family home and was never seen again. Family rumour suggests that he had a second family somewhere in Surrey. Beatrice was left to bring up six children on her own, one of whom was unable to walk. Without the financial support of her father; who had an army pension, the family would have been destitute.

There are no photos of Henry Lines in this book, and nobody from my generation has ever seen one. Beatrice must have burnt them all, or torn them to shreds. This picture shows Beatrice with her six children. Kathy is on the left:

Kathy was a talented needlewoman. She left school at fourteen and worked as a tailoress until she married. Her first job lasted one year, as did her second job and then her third. When she was sacked for the third time she asked her employer why she was being dismissed, and she was told that the boss had found out that due to her disability, the employer would have to pay extra national insurance contributions, backdated to the day that she started.

National Insurance in the 1930s was a payment made by the employer to the government to provide compensation for its employees in the event of an industrial injury, and no doubt some government actuary had decided that disabled workers were a higher risk and had to pay higher contributions. Kathy's employer said that he couldn't afford to pay that. Somebody else could do the job more cheaply. She had to go. She therefore came to an arrangement that she would reimburse the firm for the extra national insurance stamp.

She did this for ten years until the start of World War II, and she recorded all the payments she made in a series of notebooks. In 1938 she attended one of the first meetings of what became the British Polio Fellowship, a self-help organisation for people with her disability. A few years later the Polio Fellowship submitted these notebooks as evidence to the Beveridge Commission, and the national insurance rules were changed.

Kathy was very proud that her evidence had been presented to Lord Beveridge. He was one of her heroes. His report had transformed the lives of people like her, and she had played a part in the process. She had two other heroes - Franklin D. Roosevelt and my dad.

This photograph is provided by courtesy of the Franklin D. Roosevelt Presidential Library and Museum, Hyde Park, New York.

CHAPTER 4

Inspiration

In 1921, Franklin D. Roosevelt, then aged 39, had just been defeated as the Democratic Party's vice-presidential candidate. While he was on vacation at Campobello Island, New Brunswick, Canada, he was struck by a flu-like illness. It was Polio, and he was left permanently paralysed in both legs. For the rest of his life he used leg-irons and crutches to walk around the house and a wheelchair outside. He of course resumed his political career and went on to be elected President of the United States four times, from 1932 until his death in 1945.

Whilst he was running for election he let it be known that he had had Polio, and he raised hundreds of millions of dollars for medical research into the condition. But he felt that if the voters knew the true extent of his disability he would be unelectable. If he had to make a speech he would ensure that the podium was only a few feet from somewhere where his wheelchair could be hidden, and, so that he would not be seen using crutches, he would walk the few steps to the podium holding on to his son's arm.

By 1995 the FDR Presidential Library had over 35,000 still photographs and countless newsreels of Roosevelt. Only two of those photos showed him in a wheelchair, and none of the newsreels showed him being lifted, carried or pushed. Cartoonists usually portrayed him as a man of action – running, jumping, doing things. The way that the FDR political machine concealed the extent of his disabilities has been described by Hugh Gregory Gallagher, one of his biographers, as 'FDR's Splendid Deception'. Gallagher published his book that year, and largely as a result of Gallagher's campaigning, the library now holds many more pictures of the president in his wheelchair.

Roosevelt never deceived Kathy though. Whenever old newsreels of him were shown on television she would always spot the leg irons or the fact that he was supported by - not standing at - the podium. She was proud of him; he inspired her. There he was, a man in a wheelchair, a Polio survivor just like her, leading the most powerful nation in the world at the time of the greatest struggle in its history. Anything was possible.

Roosevelt inspired other people with Polio. In 1939 Frederic Morena and Patricia Carey founded the Infantile Paralysis Fellowship, which later became the British Polio Fellowship. The Fellowship was a new type of charity.

Anybody could join and able-bodied volunteers were welcome, but only people who were disabled by Polio could hold office or vote at formal meetings. Earlier charities, such as the Edmonton Cripple Parlour were founded by the 'great and the good', and dispensed charity to 'the needy'. The Polio Fellowship was based on principles that turned that idea on its head. Kathy attended one of the very first meetings in Frederic Morena's flat, and the charity was to play a very important role in both Kathy and Charlie's lives.

Neither Kathy nor Charlie stayed at Dovercourt for more than a few weeks. They found the atmosphere patronising and condescending. They were being treated as if they had learning disabilities as well as physical disabilities, and this was something they were not used to. But there was another good reason to leave Dovercourt. Charlie had had a letter from the Ministry of Labour. He had been conscripted into the labour force to work in a munitions factory in Edmonton. For the first time in his life, society wanted him and needed him to play a part, and so he went back to live at Jack's house and worked in a factory making bomber parts for the next five years.

Kathy left Dovercourt soon after Charlie. She had found work as a seamstress at Hurst Lea, a residential school for disabled boys in Sevenoaks, Kent. She lived in, and worked on making and repairing clothes for the boys. Many of the domestic staff at Hurst Lea had disabilities, as this picture shows. Kathy is in the back row on the right.

While she was at Hurst Lea she and Charlie wrote to each other, and he often visited Sevenoaks at the weekends. To get there he would have to get on a train at Lower Edmonton station in his hand propelled invalid tricycle. There's a picture of this type of wheelchair in the next chapter. It was a very heavy, long wheelbase tricycle that was operated by pulling two levers (fulfilling the same function as bike pedals) that connected to a gearbox that turned the wheels. Although they've disappeared from the streets of Europe and America, if you travel to China or India you can still see these low cost vehicles in use today.

There was no space for the trike in a regular carriage, so the trike, with Charlie in it, had to go in the guards van. When he got to Liverpool Street he would pedal his trike to London Bridge to catch the train for Sevenoaks. He was put in the guards van again, with the cargo. Kathy also travelled to Edmonton many times in the same way, and she often took him to meet her mother and sisters in Wandsworth. This journey involved pedalling the trike the three miles from Liverpool Street to Waterloo to catch the next train.

R. E. WILTSHIRE   EDMONTON, N.18.

CHAPTER 5

Charlie and Kathy

Kathy and Charlie married in May 1945, and went to live at Jack's house on Chiswick Road, Edmonton. Beatrice, Kathy's mother, was initially opposed, as she was concerned that they wouldn't be able to support themselves. She made Kathy's sisters laugh when she told them that he 'wouldn't be able to keep her in knickers.' This was a reference to the fact that the hard edges on top of the leg-irons she had to use caused her underwear to fray quickly.

Shortly after they married Charlie lost his job in the munitions factory and he was unemployed for several months. Someone told him that the British Oxygen Company, one of Edmonton's largest employers, was recruiting for assembly line work. This was 1946, and now, because there were a large number of ex-soldiers with disabilities, employers were legally obliged to offer a quota of jobs to disabled people. Charlie went to the factory on Angel Road and offered his services. He was told that they did have a job for him but that he had to be referred to them by a Ministry of Labour official, called a Disablement Resettlement Officer, those were the rules. So Charlie got back on his trike and pedalled two miles to the Labour Exchange.

He couldn't get into the office because it was up several stairs, so he asked a passer-by to go in and ask the official to come out to the Street to meet him. The passer-by returned to say that the official wouldn't come out, he was too busy, and to come back another time.

He went back the following day. This time the official did come out and told him that he knew all about the jobs the British Oxygen Company had on offer, and in his opinion Charlie was too heavily disabled for any of them. Charlie replied that he'd already been to see the company, and they didn't think he was too disabled; they just needed the right paperwork. Besides he'd been doing a similar job for the past four years. This plea was rejected, so he went back to the company who told him once more that they wanted him, but he had to get the right documents.

For several weeks he went to and fro between the company and the labour exchange. On his last visit the official was too busy to see him again.

Charlie picked up a bag of pebbles from the bottom of his trike and began to lob pebbles at the window. Not to break the window, but to make a noise to attract the attention of the people inside. Finally the official came out to see him, sighed deeply and returned inside the building to fill out the required form. Charlie started at the British Oxygen Company the following week.

Things were not easy at home on Chiswick Road. Jack had been conscripted into the army in 1940, and served in North Africa and Europe. He didn't return home for four years. In 1942 Jack's wife, Edith, died of cancer, leaving three children without their parents. Jack's requests for compassionate leave or a compassionate discharge were rejected. Their two daughters, Kath, twelve and Alma, eight, were taken in by Jack and Charlie's sister Dolly, and their ten year old son Eric was brought up by Charlie.

When Jack returned from the war he found his brother and a sister-in-law that he'd never met living in his house, effectively preventing him from re-uniting his children under the same roof. Charlie and Kathy lived in the front room and washed in the kitchen. They, like Jack and Eric, used the outside toilet, but they couldn't get to it if there was snow on the ground, as the danger of slipping over was too great. If Kathy fell, she could pick herself up, but if Charlie fell he had to be picked up. They asked the local authority to re-house them, and eventually they were, but not until 1950 when I was eighteen months old. Finally Jack was able to re-unite his family.

CHAPTER 6

Charlie, Kathy and Andrew
Family life 1948-1957

I was born in the North Middlesex Hospital on August 30th, 1948. This means that I am the same age as the National Health Service. For Kathy and Charlie, the birth of the welfare state meant that they no longer had to pay for crutches, leg irons and wheelchairs. Charlie and Mr Street could keep up their correspondence but now they wrote to each other as equals.

In 1950 Edmonton Council rehoused our family in a prefab in Sebastopol Road. Sebastopol Road was half-way between Angel Road, the industrial area, and Edmonton Green, the main shopping centre. This area had been heavily bombed in the war and many hundreds of houses had been flattened. Because of the housing shortages, between 1946 and 1954 local councils in the big cities erected over 150,000 factory built prefabs - temporary homes - and we lived in one of these. They were bungalows, so Kathy and Charlie didn't have to go upstairs. Prefabs also had inside toilets and bathrooms which were far from common in working peoples' homes at that time. They came supplied with a cooker and fridge and built-in kitchen cupboards, which meant that Kathy and Charlie didn't have to buy these things - this was essential as they quite simply didn't have the money.

The prefabs were built on land that had been bombed, although they didn't cover the entire bombed area. There were still a few Victorian terraced houses standing, but many more of them had been reduced to shattered hulks peering out from high weeds. These bombsites were just a few yards from where we lived. I remember playing on the bombsites as a five year old. Presumably it was dangerous, but all the kids played there and none of the adults seemed to mind, Kathy and Charlie included. Bombsites were exciting places to play. You could imagine you were soldiers and re-fight World War II, or be cowboys and Indians. My playmates and I were totally unaware of the human tragedies that these wrecked homes must have represented. They were just fun places to play.

My memories of what our first home looked like are very hazy. At the Chiltern Open Air Museum in Buckinghamshire you can go inside a prefab. I went to the museum to research this book and was shocked to find out how tiny they were. They were made of a steel frame, on to which asbestos concrete panels were bolted to form the outside walls, and plasterboard formed the inside walls. According to the museum, none of them were wallpapered because paper was strictly rationed. And there were no carpets or lino, just wooden floors stained brown. When I saw these wooden floors I remembered that I used to watch Charlie sitting by the fire making rag rugs in the evenings. Rag rugs are made by poking colourful scraps of textiles through a piece of hessian, knotting the underside and then sheering the top side to a uniform length. In the days of shortages and rationing they were a very cheap way of making floor coverings from recycled material.

The kitchen in the museum's prefab is exactly as I remember our kitchen in Sebastopol Road. One wall was taken up by a wooden work surface with a butler sink, and under the work service were a tiny cooker and even tinier fridge, as well as the galvanised boiler that was used to wash clothes. Just by the window was the mangle that was used to wring the laundry dry.

The prefab had a large garden that Kathy and Charlie tended part of from their wheelchairs. They grew flowers and vegetables. A larger part was left wild because it was just too big for them to cope with. Jacko the rabbit and Timmy the tortoise lived in the garden; Charlie kept pets all his life. There were two wooden sheds that the council built to house the latest innovation – motorised trikes.

The government was now issuing specially designed three-wheeled motor vehicles to disabled people. They were called invalid tricycles, and all their users knew them as trikes. Trikes seated only one person, had a two-stroke petrol engine and could reach all of 35 miles per hour on flat roads. Kathy and Charlie both passed their driving tests and the motor trikes gave them a completely new level of mobility. Charlie no longer had to pedal his way to work. Of course it was illegal to carry passengers in these motor trikes, but there was just enough room for one small boy by his dad's side:

ANDREW BRADFORD

In 1950 the Infantile Paralysis Fellowship published a fund raising brochure, and our family featured on page three:

The Heroic Story of Charles Bradford

Charles Bradford was two, and he'd just learnt to toddle. Gleefully he stumbled across the room—supported by the table and abounding confidence. Then came polio, like a thief in the night, robbing him of the use of his legs.

Charles Bradford is now forty-four. His wife, too, is a polio victim—she contracted her infirmity at the age of ten months. Nevertheless, between them they have created the kind of life which, as Bradford puts it, " springs from a contented mind."

Before the war Bradford peddled sweets from a wheel-chair. Now he has a secure job with the British Oxygen Company. In spite of his disability, he holds down his position by sheer merit.

Home from work by motor-chair, with his wife and their two-year-old son Andrew to greet him. The Bradfords were married in 1944.

Before supper there's time for a game with Andrew. Each year the Bradfords rely on the Infantile Paralysis Fellowship for their holiday arrangements.

Mrs. Bradford manages to run the home and look after Andrew in spite of her disability. They live in a pre-fab which the Infantile Paralysis Fellowship helped to obtain for them.

The national press picked up on this story, and 'The People' newspaper printed an article about us in November 1950. I would not see this article for sixty years, as nobody kept a copy of it. This publicity had some unwelcome and unexpected consequences. The old man who sold the Evening News at the bottom of our street read it, and not only verbally abused Charlie for bringing up a child that would grow up crippled, but also spat at him.

Daniel M. Angel had a different reaction. Angel, a highly successful British film producer (he produced 'Reach for the Sky', the British Film of the Year in 1956); was himself paralysed by Polio. When he read the article he offered to pay for my education at a public school. A boarding school of course.

Kathy was furious at Angel's well-meaning intervention. She took it as a personal criticism; he must be saying that she was not capable of looking after her son. She was highly sensitive to any actual or imagined accusation of that sort, and went out of her way not to ask me to help around the house. She would do it all; she would never be accused of having a child just so that he could be a carer or helper.

I like to fantasise that had Kathy taken a different view I might now be an Old Etonian or something. But I don't think it would have worked, because the contrast between the way my family lived, and the way that my fellow pupils' families lived would have been too extraordinary.

Kathy did have some help around the house though. The local council social services department provided a 'home help' to assist with housework and laundry, but

Kathy did all the cooking and shopping. Over the years she had many different home helps. Some stayed for many years and became personal friends.

ANDREW BRADFORD

CHAPTER 7

Live Eels and Grand Pianos

Kathy did her shopping on Edmonton Green in the hand-propelled trike. When I was little I went with her. The Green was a street market that surrounded two grassy triangles next to Lower Edmonton Station, and the street market was surrounded by a number of small shops and very large pubs that were very old. It was bulldozed in the 1970s and replaced by a number of undistinguished tower blocks and a bleak, soulless shopping centre. It's not now a place where you want to linger.

The heart of the Green was the fruit and vegetable market. The stalls were run by a number of dynasties that had owned them for many years; these dynasties had names like Jiggins's, Letherbarrow's and Boney's. Old Boney (I don't remember him) was a contemporary of my grandfather, William Bradford. Both of them were farm boys from Brent Pelham who had walked to London as teenagers in the 1890s, and the first place they came to in London was Edmonton, so that's where they stayed for the rest of their lives.

Young Boney ran the stall, and nobody was more inappropriately nicknamed than *Young* Boney. No matter what the weather he always wore an enormous brown overcoat, brown woollen mittens, and a flat cap. He'd lost the belt to his overcoat, so it was tied up with a rope. He would shout his wares louder than any other stallholder. 'Lovely caulies, ladies! Come and get your caulies! Best caulies in town!'

Young Boney only had one tooth. It was right in the centre of his top jaw and it was the longest and brownest tooth I've ever seen. It was the same colour as the potatoes he sold. If I had the talent to draw cartoons, the only features I would draw would be a flat cap and a single brown tooth.

Kathy couldn't get her trike into any of the shops, so she'd wait outside and ask passers by to ask the shopkeepers to come out to serve her, which in general they did willingly. So I spent lots of time waiting outside the shops with her, taking in the sights, sounds and smells of the Green.

Outside Linwood's, the fish shop, were four metal tanks containing live eels. When a woman – and all food shoppers were women in the 1950s – asked for eels, the shopkeeper would put on a pair of long rubber gloves, plunge his hand into the wriggling mass, pull out a handful and take them inside, squirming and fighting for breath. Occasionally he'd drop one, and the fugitive would hit the pavement, find the gutter, wriggle to the nearest drain and disappear out of sight. I like to think that it found its way from the drain across the Atlantic to the Sargasso Sea to spawn, but I doubt that it did.

Those that didn't escape the shopkeeper would put on a chopping block and decapitate cleanly, without fuss. While the bodies were still squirming, as they didn't yet realise they'd been beheaded, he'd wrap them up in yesterday's newspaper, hand the package to his customer, and sweep the heads into the bin.

One day I saw him put his hand into the writhing silver shoal and as he withdrew it, an eel attacked him. It managed to get its head up to the fleshy part of his forearm, just above the line of the glove, and sank its teeth in. It drew blood, but it didn't make any difference. A few seconds later it was dead.

Just down the road from Linwood's was Mansfield's wool shop where Kathy was a frequent customer. She made all her own clothes, most of mine and quite a lot of Charlie's. Mansfield's sold dressmakers' patterns, and a trip to this shop could take a long time. She had to explain what kind of pattern she was looking for, the shopkeeper would then go back inside to find it, they'd then discuss it and the shopkeeper would go back in to find an alternative.

Mansfield's was a riot of colour. The colours of the fruit and veg stalls a few feet away were mainly green, brown, red and orange but Mansfield's added blue, yellow, pink, black and grey to the palette of everyday life.

Further down the street was Firth Brothers Piano Studios, a very old building with an art deco shop front with curved glass windows, where upright and grand pianos were made, restored and sold. Firth Brothers was more appropriate to the West End than Edmonton and I can only assume it got it's customers from further afield. When I was eleven I took my grade one piano examination in this shop. We'd moved from the prefab by then into somewhere a bit bigger, and I'd asked Kathy and Charlie if they could get a piano. And they did, but not from Firth Brothers. Our piano came from the scouts' jumble sale and cost two shillings and sixpence. It was delivered on a handcart.

You can no longer buy live eels or grand pianos on Edmonton Green, but you can get a wheelchair into both Asda and Tesco, and it has more pound shops than anywhere else I know. The fruit and veg market has moved indoors and many of the stallholders are now Turkish, Indian or West Indian. Letherbarrows survives, but Young Boney has long gone.

ANDREW BRADFORD

CHAPTER 8

Auntie Floss

Auntie Floss was Charlie's oldest sister, she was born in 1898. Although she passed the entrance exam to go to grammar school, her parents didn't send her there because they didn't think that girls needed education. So she left school at fourteen and was apprenticed as a bookbinder at A.W. Bain and Co in Bethnal Green, where she stayed for over fifty years.

In the beginning, she sewed hardback books together by hand. By the time I knew her, there were machines to do that, and her job was the collator. That's the person who ensures that the pages are bound together the right way up and in the right order. She used to bring me an inexhaustible supply of drawing paper which the factory was going to scrap, and sometimes she would use surplus stocks of unbound pages to make an extra copy of a new book, just for me. She would sew the pages together herself and make the covers out of cardboard.

There were so many places that my parents couldn't take me when I was a young boy, so Floss stepped in. She took me to The Tower of London, Westminster Abbey, The British Museum and St Paul's to name but a few places. When I had to do a junior school project on the shipping industry, she took me to Cockspur Street in the West End and we collected brochures from companies such as P&O, Cunard and Canadian Pacific. Many of these brochures offered assisted passage to Australia for ten pounds. I think Floss and I collected more information than the rest of the class put together.

The great annual trip was to the pantomime at the London Palladium. We'd go to a Saturday matinee with her constant companion, Auntie Nellie, and Nellie's two nephews John and Richard, and afterwards we'd go to Lyons Corner House for high tea.

Auntie Floss lived with Auntie Nellie in a Victorian terraced house in Lion Road for over forty years, and they were devoted to each other. They owned the house; they were the only relatives I had who owned their own home in the 1950s. It was full of art deco objects and bookshelf after bookshelf of devotional literature. By the side of Nellie's armchair in the living room were her tambourines and her concertina.

Floss and Nellie met at the Salvation Army Citadel in Fore Street. On Saturday nights Nellie would preach by the war memorial on Edmonton Green. She was a real firebrand, passionate lay preacher. After Nellie had given a sermon and lead the small crowd in a hymn accompanied by her concertina, Floss and Nellie would both go into the pubs, in uniform, to sell the 'War Cry' magazine. Of course they never touched alcohol or tobacco, nor did they dance, and on Sundays they wouldn't buy a paper, switch on the radio or TV, or take a bus. This was because Sunday was the Lord's Day, and to do of these things meant that somebody else would have to work on that special day. This was against their principles and beliefs.

It was very hard for Floss not to be able to watch Sunday Night at the London Palladium, because she'd taught Bruce Forsyth at Sunday school, and she was very proud of him. When she came to our house for tea on Monday she'd ask about the show, and we'd have to tell her what had happened, and what Bruce had said or done.

Sometimes I would stay with Floss and Nellie for the weekend, and they would take me to the Salvation Army service on Sunday morning. It wasn't like the Sunday school that I went to, because their church had a big brass band and the ladies in the upper circle banged tambourines and shouted 'Hallelujah' whenever they felt like it.

Nobody crashed the tambourine more rhythmically, or hallelujahed more loudly than Nellie. I told her once that I'd never heard church music like this, and she said that General Booth (the Salvation Army's founder) had said 'Why should the devil have all the best tunes?'

When the band marched through the streets they followed two flags. One was the Union Jack and the other was a yellow star on a bright red background, and inside the star were the words 'Blood and Fire.' That's the Army's motto – it stands for the blood of Jesus and the fire of the Holy Spirit.

When I decided that I didn't believe in a god, at the age of fourteen, it must have been a bitter disappointment to Auntie Floss. Although I've been an agnostic ever since I was old enough to make the choice, Floss's church is a valuable part of my heritage.

In the school summer holidays Floss would buy Green Rover tickets that offered unlimited travel on the London Country Buses, and we'd go to places like St. Albans and Windsor Castle. One year we went to Brent Pelham for the weekend and stayed with Floss's and Charlie's Aunt Ethel and her sons on the family farm. Floss bought me my first watch and my first Brownie 127 camera.

Every Monday and Friday Floss would call into our house for tea on the way home from work. She started doing this when I was a baby, because she felt the need to call in to see if everything was alright. A light bulb might need to be changed, or the coal scuttles might need filling up, or the dustbin had to be put out. All of these things were difficult for Charlie and Kathy, and she was there to do these simple but essential tasks for her youngest brother and his wife.

Floss was a unifying force in the wider family. Relations between Jack and Charlie were strained for many years as a result of Jack's frustration at not being able to re-unite his children because his brother's family were occupying his ground floor. But when Jack married Violet in the early

1950s Floss and Violet re-united the two brothers.

The picture of Floss and Nellie at the start of this Chapter was taken at my wedding in 1978. Floss is on the right.

CHAPTER 9

Primary Schools

I started at Brettenham Road Infants School in the spring of 1953, and I still have the coronation drinking glass that was given to all school pupils in Edmonton that summer. I have hazy memories of a street party to celebrate the coronation. I remember learning to read, and I remember that Kathy used to take me there and bring me home in her hand-propelled trike. It was only a few hundred yards.

Two years later I moved next door to Brettenham Road Junior. This school, like its infants' counterpart, was a Victorian red-brick edifice with several steps to the front door. When I was there each classroom still had a coal fire and was lit by gas mantles. On winter afternoons the caretaker used to come into each classroom with a lamp on a pole to light the mantles. Nothing about the building had changed for half a century or more.

The type of education that the school provided was still pretty Victorian too. My class teacher when I was in the second year (year four in modern parlance) was Mr Davies.

I know that when you're eight years old everybody seems very old, but Mr Davies *was* very old. So old that he had attended the school as a pupil and then he had become an apprentice teacher at the same school when he was fourteen. He must have told his class that story at least once a week. No training college for him, he had spent his entire life at Brettenham and he knew nothing else. He was still teaching the way he had been taught half a century earlier. Short, round and bald, he wore trousers with a waistband that almost reached his armpits. He drove a really wonderful car though, a very large 1930s Lanchester. I was a car fanatic and I knew that Lanchesters were just as good as Jaguars or Daimlers.

I never met a fellow pupil who didn't loathe him as much as I did. Most of us were frightened of him. I only remember the detail of a few lessons. According to Mr Davies, the sun would never set on the British Empire, most of the map of the world was covered red, Rutland was the smallest county in England, Yorkshire the largest; and the people of Glasgow were very poor and it was their own fault because they drank too much and lived like pigs. Every day there was some kind of bullying tirade, usually directed at some group of people – such as Glaswegians – who these eight year old Londoners had never come into contact with; but sometimes it was directed at his pupils.

One day it was my turn. My handwriting was appalling; I have to admit it. He'd given us an exercise to write in our notebooks and when he was walking round the class he'd seen my writing - spidery and blotted - and decided to make an example of me. He made me stand on the desk while he passed my notebook around for other pupils to take a look at. He asked them to say what they thought of it. There was silence. Nobody ventured an opinion because we all knew that to do so in Mr Davies's class could have unforeseen consequences. So he told the class his opinion. This was the work of a dirty filthy pig. I had to remain standing on the desk for the rest of the lesson.

Somehow Kathy and Charlie found out about what happened. I don't remember how. I presume that when we were having tea together I wasn't my usual self and they could see that something was wrong. I imagine that they had to drag it out of me, because I was ashamed. I didn't want to tell them. Or perhaps a fellow pupil had told his or her mum and she had told Kathy. No matter, they found out and decided that they had to do something.

Usually I walked home from school; it wasn't far and there was little traffic. But as I left the school the following day I saw Charlie in his motor trike parked outside the main entrance. I was surprised. He hadn't told me he was coming to school. If Charlie or Kathy had been coming to the school on some kind of routine business, they would have just sent me back into the building to ask whoever they wanted to see to come out to the street to talk to them. But today, Charlie needed to make a point.

He repeated the trick that he had used to attract the

attention of the Ministry of Labour official ten years earlier. He started to lob pebbles at the school window. Eventually a woman teacher looked out. She seemed puzzled. She disappeared back into the room and came back to the window again with Mr Davies. The two of them looked out with furrowed brows.

More pebbles were thrown. They made a clattering noise.

Eventually Mr Davies came out. I wish I could remember the actual words they exchanged, but half a century later I don't. I looked on with a mixture of childish embarrassment and amazement. I'd never seen my dad do anything like this before. Charlie asked Davies whether he called me a dirty filthy pig. Davies evaded the question and said that he had to make an example of bad handwriting. Charlie asked the question again and Davies evaded it again. Finally, Charlie told him never, ever, to use such abusive language to his son again, and Davies neither denied that he had nor did he admit it.

I am sure that being berated by a parent was nothing new to Mr Davies. He probably enjoyed it most of the time, as the parents at this school were generally less educated than him, less articulate and either deferential to figures of authority or unable to contain their rage. He could out-argue them. Just like the pupils, inarticulate parents were easy victims.

But now he was being scolded in the street by a man with considerable and obvious physical handicaps. He was embarrassed and was unable to fight back with his usual pugnacious style. He slunk back up the steps to the school.

I left Brettenham Road School at the end of that school year. Edmonton was changing. Bomb sites were being cleared and most of the prefabs had been demolished and replaced by new council flats. The landscape was being transformed. These new flats were five or six stories high, built of yellow bricks and set in green spaces among lawns and flowerbeds. They were examples of social housing design at its best; the bleak high-rise concrete towers would not appear until a few years later.

It was the time of the baby boom, and Brettenham School was now full to capacity. A new primary school, Fleecefield, was built directly over the road from the old school, and all children who lived south of Brettenham Road were transferred to Fleecefield. A brand new school with brand new attitudes.

The picture at the front of this chapter is Miss Agatha Jones's class at Fleecefield, and I am in the front row, fourth from the left, wearing a cardigan that Kathy knitted. I was a shy child, good at reading and writing but not so good at arithmetic, art and craft and definitely not sporty. But free of the oppression of teachers like Davies, I grew in confidence at Fleecefield.

There were forty children in Miss Jones's class. In 1959 we took the eleven plus examination that decided whether we would go to grammar school or secondary modern. Only a handful of us passed the examination; because children from our part of the borough generally did not pass this exam. It was horribly socially divisive. When I went to the grammar school later that year, most of my new classmates were from the leafier parts of the borough; Winchmore Hill, Bush Hill Park and Southgate.

Two years before I moved on to secondary school we moved house. Originally there were over a hundred prefabs in Sebastopol Road, but by 1956 there were only two left. These two last prefabs housed the families that couldn't be moved into the new flats because they couldn't cope in them. Ours was one of these families and Edie Abbot's family was the other. Edie Abbot was a war widow with two teenage children, who was becoming progressively more and more paralysed by Multiple Sclerosis. The Council had a problem, and they came up with what was a far-sighted, radical solution. They would design and build two bungalows in Claremont Street, Edmonton; specifically for the two families' needs.

CHAPTER 10

Family Life 1958-69

This picture was taken by Edmonton Borough Council to publicise the work they had done to re-house the two families. Charlie and Kathy are in their new motor trikes outside the garage attached to the Claremont Street bungalow. They're both wearing cardigans that Kathy had knitted. The trikes had changed a lot as well in the past couple of years and now had fibreglass bodies which made them fully weatherproof. They were a little faster, they could do all of forty five miles an hour on full throttle, and so we were able to go further afield. They still only had one seat, and it was still illegal to carry passengers, but Kathy and Charlie still took me with them. What else could they do?

The bungalow had a sitting room, a kitchen that was

large enough for a dining table, a bathroom and two bedrooms. There was also a door leading to the garage from the house. This meant that Charlie didn't have to go outside into the garden to open the garage door to get into the trike. So there was no longer any danger of falling over an obstacle in the garden, and no danger from slipping on ice and snow. He had, when we lived in the prefab, missed work several times in hard winters because it wasn't worth the risk. And if he missed work he wasn't paid.

Other design features included electrical points fitted at waist height and light bulb sockets that could be very gently pulled down from the ceiling to change the bulb at arm level, which would then retract themselves back to their proper height. The kitchen was custom made for Kathy's needs, and the bathroom was adapted for them.

But there was no central heating, just a single coal fireplace in the sitting room. No other rooms were heated, and the bedrooms were very cold in winter. Both Charlie and Kathy and I had electric blankets, which we needed. The coal fire was both inadequate and impractical, as it was very difficult for Kathy and Charlie to lay and light a fire and dispose of the ash. I was only nine when we moved in, and I learned to do these things later. Central heating was not installed in council houses until the mid 1970s.

Like just about everybody else in Edmonton, we used to buy our coal from Alf Goodey. Alf was Charlie's maternal cousin and he ran a coal merchant's business from a wooden hut in Lower Edmonton Station goods yard. He was the only member of my extended family who could remotely be described as an entrepreneur; as well as running the coal yard he was in partnership with his son in a motorcycle dealership, and with his daughter in a garden centre at Crews Hill, Enfield. When she wasn't saving souls by the war memorial, Auntie Nellie worked as Alf's book-keeper. The coal bill was hand-written in Nellie's immaculate copperplate hand.

Alf's brother Nobbler used to deliver our coal. I'm sure that he wasn't called Nobbler on his birth certificate, but I never heard him called by any other name. Where Alf was gregarious, loud and jolly, Nobbler was shy, taciturn and withdrawn. He used to deliver the coal in one hundredweight hessian sacks, which he would empty into the coalhole next to the front door, fold the sack and return it to his truck. After a single delivery he was of course completely covered in soot, from the top of his cloth cap to the soles of his hobnail boots. Because he was a relative, Kathy felt obliged to offer him a cup of tea, but you could hardly invite him in to drink it; you would still be cleaning up a week later. So she would ask me to take him his tea which he'd drink in the garden, squatting on his haunches. No matter how hot the tea was, Nobbler would down it in one gulp, avoiding eye contact and saying nothing other than 'Thanks mate'. Then he would stand up and exhale, loudly. As he exhaled I would be hit by the smell of hot tea mixed with soot. I don't know how Nobbler would have ever cleaned up after his day's work; there certainly weren't any facilities in Alf's wooden hut. So did he go home like that? What was his home like? I can't imagine him being married.

Pleased as they were to move into their brand new

home, Kathy and Charlie were disappointed and worried when they were told that they couldn't take the cooker and fridge from the prefab with them. These were council property and had already been sold. Furnishing the new, larger home created a financial problem for them. They managed to get a new cooker on hire purchase, but made do without a fridge for many years.

***

I started secondary school in September 1959. I went to The Latymer School in Haselbury Road; a very traditional mixed grammar school with over a thousand pupils. After I'd been there a few months all the pupils in our class were handed a note to take home to their parents. It invited them to a parents evening, and asked them to confirm whether they would attend. I took it home, and Kathy and Charlie said they'd love to attend. But how would they get in? There were steps.

The following morning I went to see my form teacher, Mr Hill. Mr Hill was a thoroughly nice man who taught geography. He was close to retirement and had taught at the school for many years. I explained the predicament. He looked shocked. He was lost for words. Finally he recovered his composure and told me I needed to speak to the deputy head. The deputy head was Mr. J. A. Morris and his you can guess his nickname without my help.

I went to Jammy's office and waited in a queue. All the boys in the queue were older than me, and most of them must have been referred to him for a transgression of some rule or other. While I waited outside I heard Jammy's raised voice, the swish of the cane, and some boys came out holding a reddened left hand in their right hand. One boy of about fourteen seemed close to tears.

Finally it was my turn. Jammy was seated at his desk, wearing an academic gown that was covered with an improbable amount of chalk dust for so early in the morning. He was one of those older men who never let their barber's trim their eyebrows; his beetle brows meandered half way up his forehead in all imaginable directions.

'Why are you here, boy?' he asked, rather more loudly than I thought necessary, as he surveyed me over his half-moon glasses.

I explained the problem.

'What's that got to do with me?' his voice was raised.

'Mr Hill sent me sir.'

'Well he shouldn't have. We have a caretaker to deal with that. Go and see Mr Miles. Go. Now. Don't bother me with these things!'

I had no idea where to find Mr. Miles but now didn't seem to be the right time or place to ask. Eventually I found him in the caretaker's cubby hole. He was sitting on a bench drinking tea, surrounded by brooms, mops and buckets. I explained the problem. He listened and asked me to follow him. We went to the main door of the school, where there were three shallow steps.

'If your mum and dad park here,' he pointed to a parking space, 'and I wait to help them out of their invalid trikes, and if I put a blackboard up these steps I could push them up the blackboard. What do you think? Will that work, son?'

I agreed it would and thanked him. As I went to leave, he asked my name and I told him.

'You must be Charlie's boy then?' he replied.

Latymer was, of course, the same school where Charlie had peddled sweets to the pupils from his trike in the 1930s, and Charlie Bradford and Willy Miles knew each other. Charlie didn't know that Willy still worked there, and if he had, it would have been difficult for him to organise the parents evening directly with Willy. The school's telephone number was ex-directory, for one thing. It just wasn't given to parents until the time came to sit GCEs. And we didn't have a phone. I only knew one home that had a phone, and that was Floss and Nellie's house. None of my parents other four brothers and four sisters had a phone until later in the sixties.

Just over the road from our bungalow was a public phone box. Charlie couldn't get into it at all, and Kathy could only get in with a struggle. She would only use it in dire emergencies. If there were any non-emergency messages that had to be delivered by phone, then I would go and make the call on their behalf. Most messages were delivered by letter, and Charlie was the letter writer in the family.

Sometimes Charlie would fall over in the house or garden and couldn't get up. By the time I was eleven, I could get him up if I was there, but there were many occasions when I wasn't. When that happened Kathy would wait outside the front door for an able-bodied male to come past, and ask him if he would come into her house to pick her husband up. As soon as I left school and earned money I paid for a phone to be connected.

Charlie and Kathy enjoyed their small garden at Claremont Street. Some of Charlie's workmates built raised flower beds so that they could tend the garden from their wheelchairs. They went to garden centres in their motor trikes and bought roses, peonies and hydrangeas, among others, and planted them in the raised beds. They swapped plants with Charlie's brother and sisters who lived nearby, grew tomato plants in grow bags and sowed lettuce seeds. I have to admit that they didn't get much help from me in this aspect of their lives, like most young boys I was not interested in gardening.

***

Latymer School used the house system, copied from the public school model, to divide its pupils into six groups that could compete with each other in athletics, team sports and other events such as debating and drama. I was in Lamb House, named after Charles Lamb, the eighteenth century English essayist and poet who lived in Edmonton.

I was sitting in a house meeting in my second year when Mrs. Werry, the housemistress, made an announcement. Each house from now on would adopt a charity. I hoped that she wasn't going to say what I thought she would. But she did. Lamb House would adopt the Enfield branch of the British Polio Fellowship. My heart sank. The fellowship was a key part of our family's social life, we went to all of their meetings; and now we, my family, were going to be adopted as a charity by my school mates. It was the last thing that my twelve year old self wanted.

Mrs. Werry went on to describe the terrible situation that the people who she called 'victims' of Polio had to endure. I can't recall exactly what she said fifty years later, but I didn't recognise this portrait of my parents and their friends. I was probably being grossly over-sensitive, but what she seemed to be offering was pity, not practical support. The kind of help that made the donor feel better, but didn't really do much for the beneficiary. Whatever Kathy and Charlie were, they weren't victims. I made my mind up. After the meeting was over I went to see her and told her about our family, and asked if I could speak to the house about living with Polio at the next meeting. She readily agreed, and I went home and prepared a public speech. I discussed what I should say with Kathy and Charlie.

I had never attempted anything like this before. But the next month I spoke to about one hundred and fifty pupils aged from eleven to eighteen about what caused Polio, what help Polio survivors needed and what the Fellowship did. I don't remember much of what I said, or how long I spoke for, but I do remember saying contrary to a popular misconception – Polio was categorically not hereditary.

Mrs. Werry did me a great favour. This shy, awkward, retiring boy found that he enjoyed public speaking, and was actually quite good at it. As I moved up through the school years I started to enjoy and take part in school plays, the literary and debating society, and school politics. When the school held a mock election to co-incide with the General Election of 1964, I stood as the Liberal Party candidate. I joined the young Liberals and honed my debating skills further. Almost all of the jobs I have held as an adult have required me to make presentations, or speak at conferences, and it was at Lamb House that I first began to acquire these skills.

I probably did Iris Werry an injustice. After she retired she worked as a volunteer for the Polio fellowship for many years, and she and her husband and Kathy and Charlie got to know each other quite well. I really doubt now, having known her when I was an adult, whether she was as patronising in that first meeting as I perceived. It was probably just my youthful sensitivity.

CHAPTER 11

Work

The British Oxygen Company occupied a sprawling group of factory buildings covering several acres next to the River Lea in Angel Road. It employed over 1,300 people at its peak. Many of my classmates' dads, as well as a few mums, worked there. BOC supplied industrial gases such as Oxygen, Nitrogen and Helium to industry and the medical profession, and manufactured devices such as gas cylinders and pressure gauges that enabled their customers to use those gases.

Charlie worked on an assembly line soldering the cylinder stem (the pipe that connected the cylinder) to the pressure gauge. He worked on 'piecework', that is to say that he was paid a small basic wage and an additional amount for each gauge he produced. He never earned a lot as his disabilities prevented him from producing as many pieces as his workmates.

Like all manual workers at the time, Charlie was paid in cash every Friday. As soon as he came home on a Friday night he and Kathy would do the household accounts. He would open his wage packet, and they would set aside the exact amounts they needed for rent, insurance premiums, and the bill for the home help. Next, they discussed the estimated amount that they needed to put aside for the electricity and coal bills. When they had reached agreement they used to put this combined sum into a tin box that was kept in the kitchen cupboard next to the custard powder. It was the nearest thing they had to a bank account. Charlie kept back a tiny amount for himself and gave the rest to Kathy. What ever was left over was what we used to pay for food and whatever other expenses we had that week.

Another reason why Charlie never earned very much was that he had a lot of sickness. Polio had left him with a horribly twisted spine, which meant that he had reduced lung capacity, so he was very vulnerable to chest infections. He had at least one every winter which led to two or three weeks off work. He wasn't paid when he wasn't there.

He had a duodenal ulcer which caused him to have several months off work in one particular year, during which time he nearly died; and he also lost several months off work in 1956 with a skin condition that was caused by working with chemicals at the factory. The BOC was heavily unionised, and his union, the Amalgamated Engineering Union, fought his case for compensation from the company. He won, and with the compensation Charlie and Kathy bought their first television.

When he was off sick and wasn't being paid he applied for National Assistance – the forerunner of today's invalidity benefit - and a benefit officer would visit our house to ascertain the family's incomings and outgoings. The benefit officer then made a decision about how much state support they would get, and they would eventually receive a weekly voucher that they could exchange for cash at the Post Office.

Charlie's weekdays began at 5.30am when the alarm went off. He had to dress himself and put on his spinal corset, leg irons and surgical boots. He couldn't do this unaided, so Kathy woke at the same time and helped him. The whole process took well over half an hour. He then walked to the bathroom to wash, and to the kitchen to make tea and toast. This walk, no more than a few yards, took several minutes. Next, he walked to the garage to get into his motor trike. He needed help to get into the trike so Kathy or I used to help him by swinging his legs into the correct position when he was seated.

It was only a few minutes drive to the factory, but there were no parking places near his building, so he was allocated a shed about one hundred yards away. In the shed he kept a hand-propelled trike, and George Stevens (on the right in the picture) met him there to help him transfer into it. When he reached his building he transferred, with George's help again, to an electric wheelchair that he used on the assembly line. Electric wheelchairs weren't available on the NHS at that time;

he'd bought this one himself with the help of a small grant from the Polio Fellowship. He started work at 7.30am and finished at 4.30pm. When I was a teenager I used to open the garage doors for him at about 5pm and listen for the sound of the trike engine. When he had parked I used to open the trike door, help him swing his legs through ninety degrees, straighten them and help to swing him onto his crutches so that he could make the long walk into the kitchen.

To supplement the family income, Kathy often took in homework. The Lea Valley towns of Edmonton, Tottenham and Enfield were home to many manufacturing companies, large and small, and some of these companies gave out assembly work for women to do at home. Such jobs were usually monotonous and badly paid. The first homeworking job that I can dimly remember Kathy doing, when we were still in the prefab, was assembling artists brushes for Reeves & Co. They would deliver bags of squirrel hair and metal ferrules, and they provided her with a Bunsen burner. She had to select the right quantity of squirrel hair, shape it accordingly and insert the hairs into the metal ferrule which she had heated up with the Bunsen burner. Then she plunged the ferrule into a jug of cold water so that it would contract and grip the squirrel hairs tight. I was very young at this time - we moved to Claremont Street when I was nine – and I have no memory of how much she was paid, except that she was poorly paid. Charlie would take me to bed while Kathy was sitting at the kitchen table, assembling brushes while she listened to the Archers. I imagine she worked late into the night. I have no idea how artists brushes are assembled today, but I imagine that somewhere in China or some other Eastern country, women might still be doing this work in much the same way that Kathy did over fifty years ago, and that some of these women will have disabilities and will be working from home.

At one point shortly after we had moved to the bungalow, she was desperate for work. Whether this was because Charlie had been off sick, or because of the extra expenses they had had to pay out to equip the bungalow, I'm not sure. She decided to go to look for homework, and she took me with her. This meant that we travelled the length of the Lea Valley industrial area, from Angel Road Edmonton to Ferry Lane Tottenham, about a four mile round trip. Kathy was in the hand-propelled trike, I was on foot. At each factory, I would go into the office (often this was just a gatekeeper's lodge) and tell whoever was inside that my mum was outside in her wheelchair and was wondering if they had any homework jobs. Usually the answer was an outright no, and I would go back outside to tell her and she would pedal on to the next factory gate, but at a few places people came out to talk to her and took down her name and address, and one factory offered her work.

This was the MK Electric Company. MK was Edmonton's largest employer; it had over 3,000 employees working at twelve sites in the town in the 1970s. MK made 13 amp electric plugs and the sockets into which they were fitted. Every Monday the MK van would deliver a dozen crates containing some metal components that formed part of a socket. They had been produced in some kind of a press-mould, and needed finishing by hand. So Kathy would inspect each one, and if the edges were not properly finished she would file them clean. She could barely lift the crates, the filing action turned her fingers black and made them sore, and the living-room carpet would end up covered in metal filings. At the end of the week the MK van would collect the finished work, and pay her in cash.

If she was doing any type of homework when the National Assistance assessor was expected (luckily they always made an appointment) then it had to be hidden away in my bedroom. If she had declared the meagre income she got from homework, the cut in benefit would simply have left us without enough to live on. It was one of the financial problems of disability then, and it still is now - that any attempts that people make to earn small sums of money lead to disproportionate cuts in state benefits. It's an issue that governments recognise but haven't found any way of resolving.

She didn't do the MK work for long, it was simply too hard. She carried on working at home until I was in my early twenties. The last job she had was assembling tailors' pattern books for a small family owned company, Pike & Sons, whose factory was in Park Avenue.

In the 1960s mens' suits, even some of the cheaper ones, were still often individually made to measure by craftsmen, and the customer would visit the tailor, get measured and select the suit fabric from a book of 'swotches' on the counter. The order was then sent to a factory and the suit was made-to-measure after which the customer would pick it up a few weeks later. It was these swotch books – each page was a variation of dark grey or dark blue, sometimes there was a pinstripe - that Pike's made up for customers such as Burtons. Pike's would deliver the fabric and blocks of wood to which the fabric samples had to be glued, to our house and Kathy would make them up. Then the books would go back to the factory for the covers to be added. By homeworking standards this was relatively well paid and she liked the atmosphere of the family firm, but it meant that our front room smelt of fish glue.

Kathy's passion was making hand crafted teddy bears and other stuffed animals. She was very good at it, and won awards in national competitions. She sold some of them, but mainly she made them to give away to me, her nieces and nephews and finally to her grand-children.

She won an award for this Ocelot some time in the 1970s, and we still have him. It was made from a pattern, and the instructions said that the whiskers should be made out of horse hair, and she had trouble pinning down a supply. Somebody told her that there was a stable at Tottenham Police Station. By this time we had a home phone, so she rang up the station and explained what she was looking for. A supply of horse tail hair was delivered in a squad car the following day.

In May 2010 I wrote a short story about Charlie and Kathy that was published in the Guardian 'Family' section. The newspaper forwarded a letter to me from somebody I hadn't seen for over thirty years. The writer reminded me that I had given her baby daughter one of Kathy's Rupert Bears, and he was still going strong almost forty years later.

On Wednesday 25 October 1967 Charlie and Kathy were taken in a chauffeur driven car to the Criterion Restaurant in Piccadilly for lunch. At the lunch, Charlie was presented with a gold watch to mark the fact that he had worked at the British Oxygen Company for twenty-one years. The watch was his most treasured possession, and I still have it.

The following year Charlie retired, at the age of sixty two. He was in increasingly poor health. Polio survivors like him had always been told, at the end of initial treatment, that this was the extent of both their recovery and their disability, and they would have to get on with the rest of their lives as they were. They wouldn't get any better – but they wouldn't get any worse either.

However, by the 1960s, people who had been disabled by Polio many years before, as well as people who had seemingly made complete recoveries began going to doctors with new symptoms. Most commonly these were new, progressive muscular weakness, which might occur in the muscles affected originally but might also occur in muscles that had not been affected. Other patients complained of joint pain and fatigue, or by muscle atrophy and intolerance to cold. Charlie had all these symptoms, but the condition was neither understood nor named during his lifetime. The condition is now called Post-Polio Syndrome, or PPS.

As a result of Charlie's PPS, which was complicated by angina, Kathy increasingly became his carer, a role that she undertook willingly.

CHAPTER 12

Social Life

Charlie and Kathy had an active social life. Not all of their friends had disabilities, but a large part of their social lives were centred around the Enfield branch of the Polio Fellowship, and the North London Branch of the Invalid Tricycle Association (later known as the Disabled Drivers' Association and now called Mobilise).

To some extent they socialised with other disabled people because they had something in common, especially an interest in campaigning for improved access, but they also joined these groups for practical reasons. They couldn't just decide to go out to a restaurant on the spur of the moment, it would be too complicated to organise such a trip.

The picture at the front of this chapter is of a meeting of

the Invalid Tricycle Association in the early 1950s. It looks as though it's a Christmas party, or perhaps a Coronation party.

On the third Saturday of every month over 200 people would turn up to St John's Church Hall in Dysons Road, Edmonton for a monthly social. People with disabilities arrived in motor trikes, hand propelled trikes, hand controlled cars, and by ambulance. Many of them brought able bodied friends and relatives with them. The able bodied people did the catering, helped the disabled in and out of their trikes, put the tables and chairs out and put them back again at the end.

Once a year the group would hold an annual outing to a tourist destination. In the early days these were local seaside resorts such as Southend or Clacton, but as the group grew in confidence it took its members to more exotic destinations such as Woburn Abbey, Ross on Wye and Cambridge. There were no adapted coaches with tail lifts for wheelchairs in the 1950s, so the able bodied volunteers would carry the disabled people up the steep steps of commercial coaches and swing them in to their seats. These trips took a lot of planning and research. They had to find restaurants at the destination that could take up to fifty wheelchairs and had suitable toilet facilities - in the days before disabled toilets had been invented. Not only were places with the facilities hard to find, but some restaurant owners who had them didn't want to entertain large parties of disabled people. 'It would put the regular customers off their food.'

It is hard to believe that London Zoo was not open to the

general public on Sundays in the 1950s; it was only open to members of the Zoological Society of London and their guests. One of the ITA members was a fellow of the society, and he invited the whole membership of the North London ITA once a year. He was entitled to take his guests behind the scenes at the Zoo. None of the photos survive, but I can remember stroking an Orang-utan and handling a python on one of these Sundays.

Not everybody who attended ITA was disabled by Polio; some had Multiple Sclerosis, some Cerebral Palsy and some other disabilities. Socially, they were very mixed too. Some, like Charlie, worked on assembly lines, some were professionals. Others were employed as campaigners for the charity itself. Some ran their own businesses, like Cyril Levy who served in his corner shop in Broad Lane, Tottenham, from his crutches.

Others had never worked. Phil and Essie lived in the Jewish Home for Incurables in Stamford Hill. They were in their forties, and had both lived there since they were children. They were obviously a couple, but Phil lived in the mens' dormitory and Essie in the womens' dorm. They didn't drive; they pedalled the two miles to the meeting in their hand propelled trikes.

The social mix at the Polio Fellowship, which held monthly socials at George Spicer School in Enfield, was even greater. The virus did not understand the class system; it targeted its victims randomly. Kathy and Charlie met Sir Malcolm Sargent (chief conductor of London's Proms from 1948 to 1967) on many occasions. Sargent's daughter had died of Polio when she was eighteen and he was a strong supporter of the fellowship.

Sir Graham Rowlandson was the Enfield branch president. Rowlandson was a property developer and Conservative politician who was Chairman of the Greater London Council in the 1960s. Confined to a wheelchair by Polio, he had a London home in the West End and a country house near Welwyn Garden City. He arrived at branch meetings in a chauffeur driven Rolls Royce.

About every other year Rowlandson used to invite the entire membership of the Enfield branch to his country home, where he would set up a marquee in the grounds and provide a meal. He would hire caterers to serve his guests. And of course he was a very useful asset to the branch in campaigns to improve access or benefits.

Many of the members of these clubs had children who came to the meetings. When I was a small boy there was always someone to play with at a BPF or ITA social. I can think of at least six other couples where both partners were disabled who had children. I was the oldest, not by very much, which is why our family attracted so much publicity when I was very young. As we became teenagers, most of us joined the volunteer crew, assisting with catering, helping people in and out of trikes, helping to run jumble sales.

It was at an ITA social in the 1950s that I first heard Elvis Presley and Jerry Lee Lewis. One of the disabled members was a sound engineer, and he used to act as DJ, although this was before the term DJ was invented. We didn't have a record player at home; we couldn't afford it. But I loved music. When I was thirteen I started a paper round, and bought a reel-to-reel tape recorder with my earnings, so I could record pop music from the radio. A few months later I went to an ITA jumble sale and found a record turntable, without a case, and what looked like a good quality speaker, again without a case. I bought them both for a few shillings. Auntie Floss gave me her old wind-up gramophone. The turntable I'd bought fitted the gramophone box precisely. So I discarded the old wind-up mechanism, fitted the turntable into the box, and connected it to my tape recorder which served as an amplifier. I built a case to house the speaker and connected that to the tape recorder's outlet jack. The new speaker's sound quality was a great improvement on the tape recorder. It was loud. I could now play records, just like my schoolmates. I could go with them to Dancy's record shop on the way home from school and talk to them about which records each of us would buy.

The artists I bought included Bob Dylan, Joan Baez, Pete Seeger and Woody Guthrie. This was the time of the 1960s folk revival and I was moved by the political songs. Songs that would change the world. I still am. I think my political consciousness is as a result of spending time with people who campaigned for disability rights when I was a teenager. And there were injustices and prejudices that required people to campaign.

The picture on the next page shows the ITA branch committee in the 1950s. Charlie is second from the left in the back row. There don't seem to be any women on the committee, but it was the fifties after all. In the front row, on the left is Fred Prudence. Fred was married to Joyce, who also had Polio, and they had adopted a girl of about ten; a relative of Joyce's. Fred worked for himself, as a watch repairer, from home.

In 1959 Fred and Joyce decided to buy a house in Palmers Green. They needed a mortgage, which was granted. While their house purchase was going through, some neighbours got up a petition to the Building Society. They didn't want cripples living in their street. At that time you could see advertisements in the paper: 'Room to Let. No dogs, No Irish, No coloured.' Add cripples to that list. The building society sent the protesters away. Fred and Joyce bought their house.

I first heard this story a few years later, when I was about fourteen. Kathy and Charlie had returned from a Polio Fellowship meeting, where they had met a young disabled couple who had a baby girl. The baby had short arms and legs as a result of her mother being prescribed the thalidomide drug during pregnancy. Kathy said how sad this was, because people would say that it was hereditary and they would tell the couple that they had no right to have children. I told Kathy and Charlie about the playground incident, of five years ago. I had never mentioned it to anybody before. In return Charlie told me about Fred and Joyce, and about the news vendor who had abused him on the street. That was the part that really shocked me, I knew the man he was talking about; he seemed a pleasant enough old boy to me. In my bedroom later that evening, I played Bob Dylan's 'The Times They are a-Changin'.

I remember many occasions when there was a knock on our door and a stranger would ask for Kathy and Charlie's help. The person at the door knew somebody who had just become disabled. In the 1950s this usually meant that they had had Polio, but as the vaccination program reduced the number of new cases to a trickle, the reasons for the disability changed. Increasingly, the cause was Multiple Sclerosis. Charlie and Kathy would always invite the person in and make them tea. The person would ask how they could get help? How they could go about getting a wheelchair? Was there somewhere this person could go for something to do? Charlie and Kathy would answer their questions and Charlie would write all the addresses down for them. He would ask where the person was living and whether their accommodation was accessible for him? If it was, he would usually go to see them to give them advice directly rather than through a third party.

CHAPTER 13

Out and About

The motor trikes meant that our family could go to places and see people. The longest regular journeys we made in these very basic vehicles were to Brent Pelham and Worthing.

Charlie and his brothers and sisters were the first generation of their family who were born in London. Since the early eighteenth century the Bradfords had lived in the tiny hamlet of Brent Pelham on the Hertfordshire and Essex borders. All the boys in all the generations had become farm labourers, while their sisters became domestic servants. William, Charlie's father, was the oldest child, and he was named after his father in an unbroken tradition since 1743. He had walked the 30 or so miles to Edmonton when he was a teenager, with his friend Boney, and established his horse-drawn cab business there a few years later. Charlie had been partly brought up by his grandmother in her thatched cottage in the village. I took the picture of her cottage on my last visit to Pelham with Charlie and Kathy. I was fifteen, and Auntie Floss had given me a Brownie 127 camera for my birthday.

Every year Charlie and Kathy and I would go to see Charlie's Aunt Ethel and his cousins at Pelham. Ethel was the widow of Charlie's uncle George, his father's youngest brother. George and Ethel had been landlord and landlady of the village pub, the Black Horse. The pub was built in 1597 and is still a working pub today. Every landlord of the Black Horse for two hundred years, George Bradford included, has engraved his or her name on a window in the saloon bar. The oldest inscription, signed by Jane Wright in 1801 says 'Here I stand by day and night, to sigh out cold and let in light.' I don't know where those words come from, Google doesn't produce a match. Perhaps Jane wrote them herself? None of the Bradford family could have done that in 1801. On all the birth and marriage certificates that I've seen up to William's birth in 1873, my forebears have made their mark with a cross.

In George and Ethel's time the pub was also the village bakery, and they sold bread to the villagers. At harvest time George also worked as a farm labourer on the estate of Major Barclay, the owner of Brent Pelham Hall. They rented the pub from Major Barclay as well. There was presumably hardly any economic activity in the village that Major Barclay was not involved in.

I never knew George; he died when I was three, and by

the time I knew Ethel she was in her sixties, but she was a very old sixty-year old. She had hardly ever left the village. She always spoke deferentially about Major Barclay and referred to him as 'the squire', or 'Squire Barclay'. Ethel and George had seven children, and countless grandchildren, many of whom lived in the village.

After George died Ethel and her two bachelor sons Bill and Eric, who were in their forties when I first knew them, bought 'Rectory Farm', a smallholding on the edge of the village. Our family made an annual trip to Rectory Farm every July.

It took nearly two hours in the trikes, a large part of which was spent getting up the steep Wadesmill Hill on the A10 road north of Ware. The trikes' two-stroke engines struggled with steep hills; they could barely do twenty miles an hour on an incline like Wadesmill. We travelled in convoy, Charlie's trike with me by his side, followed by Kathy's trike with Charlie's folding wheelchair at her side. We travelled this way out of necessity, but it had the advantage that if one trike broke down the other one could go for help. For this reason, both of them always kept four old pennies - the money needed to call the AA - in a pocket in their trike. In the event of a breakdown, the other trike would drive to a phone box. There weren't many phone boxes on the route to Pelham though, it was very rural. I can remember trikes breaking down in all sorts of places, but thankfully never on a Pelham trip, where getting help might have been difficult.

Because they had to take me with them it meant that wherever they went, they could only take one wheelchair.

Charlie depended entirely on a wheelchair outside of the house, but Kathy could walk short distances on crutches, so the only places we could go to were places where Kathy could manage without a wheelchair.

I loved the Pelham trips. It was another world to this urban child. The farmhouse was at some time a schoolhouse, and Ethel's very large dining room was the old school room. It was full of glass cases of stuffed animals; dogs, cats, foxes and birds, and antique china and cutlery. The dead animals had glass eyes and were mounted on branches surrounded by preserved flowers or grasses, or sat on artificial grass. The household china must have been handed down through several generations. As well as the dining room, there was a small sitting room and a rudimentary kitchen with an open range for cooking and heating.

We used to set out early and arrive shortly after ten. As soon as Kathy and Charlie had managed to get into the sitting room Ethel would make them tea, and my cousin Eric would take me round the farm. He waited until I had arrived so that I could help him collect the eggs. They kept free-range chickens in coops in the field nearest to the house, and Eric would pick up a bucket from the barn and we would go egg-collecting. The coops were large enough to walk into, and he waited outside while I went into the coops and found the eggs. The coops smelled of warm straw, the eggs were warm to the touch and the chickens would cackle and run as I went in. Egg collection finished, I'd help him feed them with prepared chicken feed supplemented by wheat from the field, lupins from the garden and scraps from the family meals. Then we would go back and fetch Charlie, and push him round the fields where the cows and pigs were grazing. Because Charlie had been brought up in a farming household, he was knowledgeable about livestock, and he used to ask questions about the breeds, and the prices the animals were fetching at Hertford market.

Then it was back to the house for lunch, cooked by Aunt Ethel. An enormous meal of home grown vegetables and home produced meats, followed by crumbles and pies made from home-grown fruit. After lunch Ethel's daughters, sons-in-law and grandchildren would drop in to see Charlie and Kathy. The kettle was filled and put on the kitchen range to make more tea. Endless cups of tea. Sometimes there were ten or more people crammed into Ethel's sitting room. I would usually go and play outside with Barbara and Sally, two grandchildren a bit younger than me. Because there were so many grandchildren, Bill and Eric had bought a pony, so I tried my hand at riding, guided by my younger cousins who were far more proficient riders than me.

Finally, it was time to go. We never went home empty-handed. We were always presented with a brace of pheasant – which was handed over a little furtively, so I imagine it was one of Major Barclay's birds - and whatever was going in the kitchen garden; usually beetroot, potatoes, broad beans and whatever fruit was in season. The trike smelled of fresh produce on the way home. The oddest thing that I ever brought back was Timmy the Tortoise. Timmy had been the pet of one of Ethel's granddaughters for twenty years. She'd found him when she was a little girl, so nobody knew how old he was. She was leaving home to get married and there was no place for Timmy in her new flat. Timmy stayed with us for about ten years until we gave him away to another small boy. Perhaps he's still alive?

As we got back into the trikes for the journey home, a crowd of Charlie's relatives would stand at the garden gate, waving us off and wishing us well. On the way home we would stop in the village, and Charlie would show me the stocks where miscreants were punished in medieval times by public humiliation. Offenders were immobilized and exposed to the scorn of passers-by. The idea was that anybody could assault, revile or aim filth at the victim. The stocks were (and still are) outside the church and opposite the village hall, and a few yards from the thatched cottage where Charlie was brought up.

The last time I made this journey I was fifteen, and could no longer fit in Charlie's trike, so I made my way by train to Bishops Stortford where Cousin Walter was a local cabbie, and he picked me up. The picture of me on the horse, with Eric holding the bridle was taken on my new camera.

***

In 1950 the Polio Fellowship opened the Lantern Hotel in Worthing, Sussex. Many of my childhood holidays were spent there. Every other year, the local branch of the Fellowship gave Charlie and Kathy a grant to pay for a two-week stay at the Lantern. The hotel offered full-board accommodation to members and their families. All its rooms were accessible to wheelchairs, as was the garden, and the town itself didn't have any steep hills, so people with disabilities could use the beach, the shops and the cafes relatively easily.

Worthing is seventy miles from Edmonton, and that was the longest journey we ever made in the motor trikes. A few weeks before we were due to set out, Charlie would write to the AA and ask them for a route map 'avoiding steep hills'. We would set off, in convoy as usual, on the Friday night and spend the night with Kathy's sister Connie and her family. When I first went to Worthing, Connie lived with her husband Tom, and three children, Coral, Heather and Paul in Routh Road, Wandsworth. The house backed on to Wandsworth Common and had six bedrooms on three floors. My Grandmother Beatrice, her two daughters Connie and Dolly and their families, and her son Dennis and his family all lived in the same house. They had all moved there when Beatrice's much more modest rented house in Southfields was badly damaged by a bomb. In wartime, local councils used to requisition empty properties to house people whose homes had been damaged, and move them in to them. Eventually the councils had to give these houses back, and Routh Road was returned to its owners in the late 1950s. Beatrice had died by then, and the three families were rehoused in much more modest council houses. Connie's family moved to Tooting, so in later years we would spend the night there. Today a Routh Road house costs over £3 million, but then it was just a council house.

We stayed with Connie's family because they lived on

the ground floor. But there were no toilets on that floor, and my cousin Heather recalls her father Tom carrying Charlie and Kathy upstairs to the toilet, and waiting outside the door to carry them down again.

On one visit to Worthing when I was still at junior school, Kathy's trike broke down at Stamford Hill, only about five miles from home. Charlie was leading the convoy with me by his side. When we realised that she wasn't with us he turned around to find her stuck at traffic lights with a couple of men pushing her into the kerb. Somebody must have phoned the AA, I don't remember who. Charlie gave me some money to buy an ice-cream, and when I returned a police constable was talking to him. He was just making sure that they were alright, and making small talk while we were waiting for the AA. As Kathy and Charlie couldn't get out of the trikes to talk to each other, he was also ferrying messages between them, and generally keeping spirits up. I hovered a few yards away, sucking on a strawberry lolly, when the policeman realised that I was something to do with the party.

'Who's this?' he asked

'Our boy.' replied Charlie

'What's your name son?'

'Andrew'

'Are you off on holiday too?'

I nodded.

'In this?' he pointed to the trike and looked at Charlie.

'I know we're not insured,' replied Charlie, 'but what else are we supposed to do?'

'Do what you have to.' replied the constable. He then

turned to me. 'Son, I'll wait here for the AA to fix this. Just don't get back in there till you see me go round the corner. If you can't see me then I can't see you either.'

The AA arrived and the problem, whatever it was, was fixed. We arrived at Routh Road a few hours late.

The Lantern was a family hotel. The guests included couples, one or both of whom had Polio, single people, and couples who had children with Polio. There were some families where the virus had attacked more than one generation. When I was eleven, we met Len S. and his family. Len's wife had died of the disease, and both of his children - a boy of twelve and a girl of ten when I met them - had caught the virus; all three of them in the same epidemic about five years earlier. His son had made a full recovery, but his daughter was left seriously handicapped. Len was now married to Kath, and one evening Kath told us how they had met. Len lived in Somerset, and his daughter was in rehab in a specialist hospital in London. He was only able to get to see her about once a month. On the train to London, he had got talking to Kath, a Londoner, who was so moved by his story that she went to visit this little girl whom she didn't know in hospital. She visited every week for months. A couple of years later Kath and Len married and Kath brought the children up as her own. She told us this story late one night when the rest of her family had gone to bed; up till then we hadn't realised that she wasn't the childrens' birth mother, and all three of us were humbled by this family's love and bravery.

There was never any shortage of other children to play with. Guests arrived by motor trike, car, train and taxi, hand propelled trikes that had been out on the train, and also by ambulance.

When the weather was fine, a party of us would walk or pedal or push someone to the hotel's beach hut. When I was old enough I'd push Charlie in an indoor wheelchair while Kathy made the journey in a hand-propelled trike that she hired from the hotel. She couldn't keep up with me, I was the fastest wheelchair pusher in Sussex. Worthing has a long tarmac promenade with no steps or bumps, so I could run with the wheelchair, then jump on the footrests at the back and free wheel for yards and yards.

At the beach, able-bodied relatives such as Len would carry any Polio survivors who wanted to swim across Worthing's stony beach into the water. There was no separation between the disabled and the volunteers; nobody even thought of themselves as volunteers. People would just muck in so that everybody had a good time.

As I grew older I became very conscious that our group were objects of curiosity. People would stop what they were doing and stare at us, open mouthed. They'd talk about us as if we couldn't hear them. I don't think I was ever embarrassed for myself, I just thought that the polio survivors I was with deserved better than to be gawped at. One day Len noticed the expression on my face as I overheard the words 'spastic' and 'ugly' from some stranger's mouth.

'Learn to ignore it, Andrew,' he said. 'Your mum and dad have dignity. If you answer back you bring yourself down to their level.'

The last time I went to the Lantern I was sixteen. I could

no longer fit in the trike, so I went by train. Most of us can remember holidays with parents at that age; it's an age when you would rather not be there. You want to be doing something different. I was no exception. The hotel seemed to be full of older people or very young children; nobody I could relate to.

Until Chantal and Genevieve turned up. Chantal was seventeen and came from Troyes in the Champagne region; Genevieve was fifteen and came from Le Mans. They'd met in an orthopaedic hospital in Paris when they were very young; Chantal had had scoliosis that had been successfully treated by surgery, and Genevieve had Polio. She wore leg irons and used two walking sticks. They had come to Worthing on their own by train, passenger ferry and taxi. When I think about it now, it was a feat of courage and endurance, for Genevieve was quite seriously disabled and very young to travel to another country. But I didn't realise it at the time.

The two girls had schoolgirl English and I had schoolboy French, thanks to Mrs. Werry. I'd never met any French people before; they seemed quite exotic to me. And I introduced them to Johnny Cash's music. On my first day in Worthing I was hanging around the shops because I had nothing better to do, and I saw Johnny's new album 'Orange Blossom Special' on sale. So I bought it. But there was nothing to play it on; the hotel didn't have a record player. But the hotel manager told me that there was a shop where you could hire one by the week, so I did. And every evening Chantal, Genevieve and I would sit in the conservatory, listening to the same twelve tracks of that deep baritone voice time and time again; until Chantal decided to buy a Francoise Hardy album to add a Gallic flavour to the evening.

Our family kept in touch with Genevieve for several years, and the year after I left school I hitch-hiked around Normandy and stayed with her and her family in Le Mans.

CHAPTER 14

Epilogue

I left school in 1966 aged eighteen, and left home three years later. Charlie became increasingly frail after he retired, as a result of Post-Polio Syndrome complicated by angina and repeated chest infections. Kathy enjoyed reasonably good health as she entered her sixties, which was fortunate as she increasingly had to spend much of her time taking care of him.

In retirement they were financially better off than they had ever been when Charlie was working, as they had the basic state pension, a small company pension, and attendance allowances. They even opened a bank account. They now had a phone, which made a transformational difference to the quality of their lives. They could talk to friends whose houses they couldn't visit, they could order goods from shops that they couldn't get into, and, above all, they could get help in emergency. Charlie would never again need to lob pebbles at windows so that he could be heard.

I paid the phone rental from the time I left school until 1970, when the Chronically Sick and Handicapped Persons Act was passed. This act obliged local authorities to provide telephones to people who were isolated as a result of their disability. When Kathy and Charlie applied for this benefit they were initially turned down because 'Claremont Street is not an isolated place.' I wrote an appeal letter, which pointed out that before they had a phone, Kathy had been often been forced to stand at the doorstep to ask passers by to come into the house to pick her husband up. Was that not a form of isolation? We won the appeal.

Motorised invalid tricycles were phased out in the 1970s and replaced by the mobility allowance and the Motability scheme which enabled users to purchase adapted cars; although neither Kathy nor Charlie ever learned to drive a car.

I married Marilyn in October 1978, and the pictures at the front of this Chapter are of Charlie and Kathy at our wedding. It is Charlie's last picture; he died of heart disease in May 1979, aged seventy-three. He died a few months after his brother Jack, and about eighteen months before his sister Floss.

Just a few weeks after Charlie died Kathy found a lump on her breast, and was successfully treated for cancer. Once she had recovered, she went on to do many things that she had been unable to do while she was Charlie's carer. She travelled abroad. She went to France, Holland and Italy on coach trips organised by the Across Trust; a charity that specialised in taking even the most seriously disabled people around the world. In Italy she was blessed by Pope John Paul II. At the age of eighty-one she flew for the first time, to Orlando on a Disneyland trip organised by the Polio Fellowship. She was close to her two granddaughters, Victoria, born in 1981 and Charlotte, born in 1983.

After she returned from Florida she became frailer. She was now diabetic, and was starting to lose sensitivity in her fingertips. This made preparing meals increasingly difficult. It also meant that she could no longer sew and knit, and make teddy bears for family and friends. Losing this ability distressed her.

Kathy went into residential care in January 1995, and died a few weeks later of heart disease. She was eighty three.

CHAPTER 15

Telling the Story of Charlie and Kathy
The Window – A Play

I first tried to write about our family in 2000, but my first attempts were not very good. They were long on facts and short on feeling. But I did do some useful research by asking older cousins about their memories of Charlie and Kathy before I was born. The demands of work meant that my writing effort was sporadic and disjointed.

In 2007 I stopped full-time work and joined the local branch of the University of the Third Age (U3A) where there is an active creative writing and poetry group, and some parts of this book were originally written as short stories that were read aloud to this group. In 2008 I entered one of these stories, 'The Window', into a competition organised by the Millfield Theatre in Edmonton. 'The Window' is based on the incident at Brettenham Junior School where Charlie came to the school to protest about the bullying teacher, but it also tells a little about Charlie and Kathy's early life.

The Millfield was developing a play called 'Tales of Edmonton' that would comprise a number of short plays about Edmonton life; and it was working with Face Front Inclusive Theatre, a mixed company of disabled and able bodied professional actors. I had never heard of Face Front, but when I looked at their website I thought that if this company can't tell this story, then nobody can.

In August the Millfield rang to say that they wanted to use my story, and a few weeks later I went to Face Front's studio at Edmonton Green for the first time. I kept a diary of the play's development, and here are some extracts:

Friday 19 September 2008:

Today I met Catrin Thomas and Shirley Mason, who are to direct the play. Catrin and Shirley explained how improvised theatre works. I am to provide the actors with information about the people and the events, and the actors, directors and the author will 'improvise' - we develop the script jointly. This makes me a little nervous, as it does mean that the author can lose control, but I'm happy to go along with it and see what happens.

I have already written the first draft of the classroom scene where I was bullied and we go through it. Shirley tells me that they also want to set another scene; back in the 1940s when Kathy and Charlie first met. The story has told them that in the 1930s Charlie ran a 'cripple parlour' and they'd like to set a scene there as well. She thinks that the very words 'cripple parlour' are so shocking to a modern audience that they will make them think. The story has also told them about Kathy's notebooks –where she recorded the fact that as a disabled person she had to pay extra national insurance in the 1930s; and Charlie's letters to potential benefactors asking for financial assistance to buy wheelchairs. Shirley and Catrin want these struggles to be dramatised. We also discuss a possible opening scene. A modern, inspirational teacher could be giving a social history lesson about people who have 'made a difference' in Edmonton, and later the same actor could transform himself into the bullying Mr. Davies.

Tuesday 7 October 2008 – Development day

Today I meet the actors who are playing Charlie and Kathy – Angus Davie and Julie Parker. Julie is profoundly deaf; she has been a member of Face Front for ten years and played in many of its productions. Angus, an actor, film-maker and disabled rights activist, uses a wheelchair outside the house, and has travelled from East Ham - in his wheelchair – by tube and train this morning. He is late. The reason that he is late is that he got to Edmonton Green Station on time and asked a member of the station staff to carry his lightweight folding wheelchair down the stairs while he (Angus) walked down the stairs. The man refused. He said it wasn't his job and he wasn't insured to do it. He told him to go to the next station where there aren't any stairs. So Angus had to phone Face Front and ask Catrin to meet him and provide him with the - very little - help that he needed. When he arrives at the studio there's some discussion as to whether really anything has changed since Charlie and Kathy's times. Charlie was able to use this station to visit Kathy in the 1940s, and he must have needed far more help than Angus did.

Shirley sees a dramatic opportunity here – can we use the character of the modern inspirational teacher to contrast disability today and yesterday?

After actor's warm-up exercises Shirley leads a workshop session where the actors and directors question me about many of the themes of this story, and my answers are written up on a whiteboard. What was Polio and how did people get it? Just how disabled were Charlie and Kathy? Where did they meet and when? What were their backgrounds and personalities? What did they like to do in their spare time? What was it like to be their son?

Most of the questions (as well as the answers) are predictable, but I find some of them more probing than I expected. I really had to think about 'who was the strongest personality' and 'what was it like to be their son?' I hadn't thought of this story as being about me at all, but of course it is about me as well as about Charlie and Kathy. Someone asked about our family's social life and I replied that many of their friends also had Polio; but because the Polio virus didn't care about social class they had friends from very wealthy and privileged backgrounds as well as working class people like themselves. Angus, who became disabled as an adult, confirmed that this was his experience too. The friends he'd made because of his disability are an equally varied bunch.

We then improvise three scenes - a scene set in the 1940s where Charlie and Kathy are introduced to the audience, a scene where Kathy and Charlie find out that their son's been bullied and a scene outside the school where Charlie confronts the teacher. I have to take detailed notes and then re-draft the script before the first rehearsal.

Monday 3 November – First Rehearsal

I meet Jan Lower for the first time. He's playing the two teachers –the inspirational modern teacher who acts as the narrator and the old bullying 1950s teacher. He improvises the modern role brilliantly. He's incorporated what happened to Angus at Edmonton Green last month into his social history lesson and I record it on a minidisk recorder, take it home and turn it into a script. His improvisation was phenomenal, far better than anything I could have written conventionally.

Monday 10 November – Second rehearsal

Everybody knows their lines now, so Catrin and Shirley are concentrating on getting the emotions right. They're working on the body language and eye contact between Kathy and Charlie, and Charlie and the old teacher. It's very interesting for me to watch and see how these ideas are developed. Having said that 'everybody knows their lines', we are still making modifications as part of the improvisation process. I do feel that it's coming together.

We're also selecting images from my family albums to project on screen and incidental music – we choose Glenn Miller for the scenes set in the 1940s and Bill Haley for the scene set in 1955.

Saturday 15 November 2008: The Performance

'Tales of Edmonton' was performed to a packed house at the Millfield Theatre, and among them are twenty four of my friends and family members, including many who knew Kathy and Charlie. At the end Marilyn tells Julie that she has captured her mother-in-law's body language exactly. On the next page there are some dress rehearsal photos.

I have continued to work as a volunteer and trustee of Face Front since the play, as I feel that I owe a lot to them, and because they use drama to work with some of the most disadvantaged people in London.

Julie Parker as Kathy, and Angus Davie as Charlie

Charlie confronts the bullying teacher

CHAPTER 16

Yesterday's News

I had never seen the article in 'The People' that caused Daniel M. Angel to offer to support me, and the news vendor to abuse Charlie. But I thought that it was essential to find it, as without evidence that it existed I would just be writing down family folklore, not real history. So I made a trip to the British Library Newspaper Archive and wrote this piece on my return:

It's only twelve miles from my home to the newspaper reading room, but my journey takes me back nearly sixty years. It isn't my first visit; I've been there before. To search for an article about my family that Kathy told me was published in one of the Sunday papers when I was very little. The trouble is, she was vague about which paper had published it. I now believe that it was 'The People' and that the article was published some time between 1949 and 1952. But I'm not wholly certain; I'm prepared to come back empty-handed yet again.

The Library's newspaper reading room is a 1930s brick-built building in Colindale, a North London suburb. It sits on a low hill opposite a row of 1930s terraced houses, an old-fashioned workmen's café and a Turkish supermarket. The traffic is heavy, and it's the hottest day of the year. As I walk uphill from the side street where I've parked I glance at my watch. Its 10.15.

I'm not looking forward to today as I'm not at all optimistic about finding this article. But inside it's air-conditioned, the staff are friendly and helpful and the four rolls of microfilm that I've ordered in advance are waiting for me. The Library's 19th Century collection has been digitized and indexed, so if I were researching something from that period I could have just done it from home, in minutes, over the internet. But the 20th Century collection is still only available on microfilm, so I take my four rolls of film to desk 111 and thread the 1949 roll into the viewer. I will spend today reading as many editions of the People as it takes.

It doesn't take that long to read a newspaper from that era, because they only had eight pages. After you've read half a dozen editions, you get to understand the structure. Page one is proper news. By the time you get to 1950 the main issues were war in Korea, food rationing, and a general election. The coverage of world and political news is far more detailed and informative than anything you would find in the same newspaper today. Sometimes Polio makes the headlines as major epidemics sweep across the country. It's a serious concern.

Page two is showbiz, page four usually serialises somebody's war memoirs and the last three pages are sports. This means that anything about our family, if it exists, would almost certainly be printed on page three or page five. I get sidetracked by the sports pages. Spurs had a brilliant season in 1949-50. Thanks to sixteen goals from Len Duquemin they were second division champions and won promotion. Next season they were first division champions for the first time in the club's history. I've met Len Duquemin. I don't remember him as a player and local hero – he retired when I was very young - but I knew him as the owner of a corner shop in Tottenham where I used to buy a paper on my way to work when I was eighteen.

I settle into a routine. A brief look at the main headlines, a detailed scan of pages three and five, read the Spurs match report, then go on to next Sunday's edition. On pages three and five I see lots of references to cripples; only one reference each to spastics and mentally retarded people, and two references to 'lame chicks'. This puzzles me; it must be something to do with disability but what? So I read these articles in full. It seems that 'lame chicks' are children with learning difficulties, and in a midlands town they're having a hard time because when a local vicar decides to let a group of them use a church hall for social events the residents protest. 'It would upset the normal boys and girls to see them.'

Some things do change in sixty years, others don't. Professional footballers no longer open corner shops when they retire, but people who look different do still face discrimination, prejudice and abuse. If you read today's newspapers you can read about disability hate crime.

Then I find an article that really shocks me. A local council in Wales is concerned. There was a US Forces base in its area during the war, and as a result it now has thirty eight 'picaninnies' in its children's homes. Nobody wants to adopt them. The council has sought a meeting with the US Embassy to get them relocated to the United States, as 'that's where they belong'.

Do they? Just where in the USA does this council expect them to go? Mansions in Beverley Hills? Penthouse apartments in Manhattan? I think it's far more likely that their American dads (if they didn't die in the war) live in sharecropper shacks in Alabama, and I doubt that mixed race Welsh children would be very welcome there. I am aghast. But I can't afford to linger over this article, I need to find the one that I came to find. This is a tale that somebody else should tell. I carry on reading.

After I've read about 100 editions of The People I get to Sunday November 5 1950. I actually jump in my seat and cry out 'Oh My God' when I see a picture of the two year-old me with Charlie and Kathy on page five. Other researchers look up as I break the silence. The headline is predictable. 'Cripples with a Wonder Baby.' But actually the article paints a positive picture. It describes Charlie and Kathy's story as one of 'courage that conquered pain, [and] determination that triumphed over difficulties.' Kathy is quoted as saying 'Our dearest wish was to have a child. Now we have Andrew we are very happy.'

How do I print this? I leave desk 111 and go to the counter to ask how. A young woman with a lyrical Dutch accent tells me that I have to open an account with the library and pay in advance; the printing machine will debit my account. I ask how much a copy costs? Twenty pence. I ask what's the minimum credit they'll accept? Twenty pence. I give her a 20p coin and she sets me up with an account number, username and password and tells me that I can check the balance of my account on the internet at any time. I doubt that I'll bother. My account is now in credit but I have to wait for half an hour before a printer is free. Then it's mission accomplished. As I start the car engine I hear the two o-clock news.

I only print this one article, and as soon as I get home I regret being so single-minded. I'm haunted by the story of the thirty eight children in Wales and I should have copied that one as well. I wonder what became of them, whether any of them have told their stories? I can't stop thinking about them. We now know of course that the people who ran children's social services in that era would do anything, no matter how inhumane, to save money, If these children had pure Welsh blood they might very well have been sent away to Australia at the age of eleven; cheap labour. They might have been told that their mothers were dead when in fact they lived round the corner. But Australia didn't want mixed race children then.

I searched the internet. No, Wales was not the only place having these conversations with the US authorities; and no, the children weren't welcome in the USA. In 1947 Congressman John E. Rankin of Mississippi said that he was 'unalterably opposed to bringing to this country a lot of illegitimate half-breed Negro children from England.' They were, he went on, 'the offspring of the scum of the British Isles.'

I found a BBC online forum of about five years ago which is now closed to new posts. Rachel James of North Carolina has posted an entry headed 'My Father's Brown Babies'. She says that her GI father had told her about two half-sisters, older than her, who he left behind in Staffordshire. He had no choice because he was seriously wounded in France and repatriated to the US, where he was in hospital for months. He never got the chance to return to England. He's been dead for many years, but she remembers him telling her how much he loved them and how beautiful they were. At the time of her post, Rachel was still searching for her half siblings so that she could tell them that he never forgot them.

If the Library's 20th Century archive had already been digitized, I would never know this story and I wouldn't remember that I knew Len Duquemin, the hero of White Hart Lane. Researching things the old-fashioned way may be more time consuming but it can be more rewarding. I feel far more in touch with the period that I'm writing about after having read 100 editions of The People than if I'd just followed an on-screen dialogue.

I showed my family the article I'd copied and suggested that they might want to call me 'Wonder Baby' in future. But nobody has.

ACKNOWLEDGEMENTS

I would like to thank everybody who has read earlier drafts of this story and encouraged me, especially everybody at Broxbourne U3A Creative Writing and Poetry Group and Bishopsgate Writers, as well as Marilyn, Victoria and Charlotte, Gill Bell, Carole Grey, Jane Thompson and Angela and Tony Tribe. Thanks also to my cousins John Webber and Neal Nicholls for their genealogical research into the Bradford and Bridgeman families, and to Mike Cliff for his help with photo manipulation. A special word of thanks to everyone at Face Front Inclusive Theatre, especially Shirley Mason, Catrin Thomas, Angus Davie and Julie Parker for making me realise that this story was also about me as well as Kathy and Charlie.

A final word of thanks to Seema Patel, my editor at Callio Press.

Andrew Bradford was born in Edmonton, North London in 1948. He is married, with two adult daughters and lives in Hertfordshire. Now semi-retired, his career was spent in information technology in the banking and investment industry, and he is the author of 'The Investment Industry for IT Practitioners: an Introductory Guide'; one of the standard textbooks on how information technology is used in the banking and investment industry.

Andrew enjoys reading, theatre, music, gardening, photography and travel as well as creative writing; and he has had articles published in 'The Guardian' and 'The Spectator'.

www.andrewbradfordauthor.com